WILD TECHELLATIONS

Coloring Book

John Wik

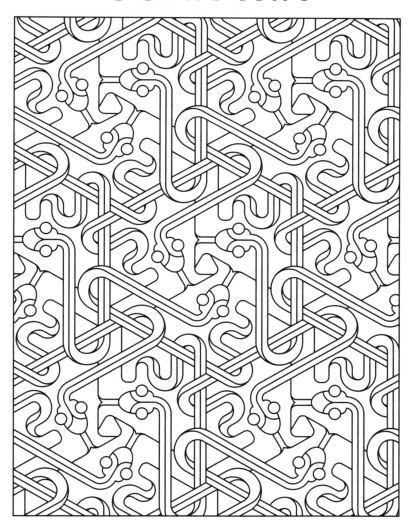

DOVER PUBLICATIONS, INC.
MINEOLA, NEW YORK

Featuring many of nature's most interesting creatures—snails, flamingos, crocodiles, and lions, among others—these exquisite designs offer the experienced colorist the creative opportunity to experiment with colored pencils, markers, or even paint. The dynamic, interlocking images are printed on unbacked, perforated sheets for easy display.

Bibliographical Note
Wild Techellations Coloring Book is a new work, first published
by Dover Publications, Inc., in 2016.

International Standard Book Number
ISBN-13: 978-0-486-80519-1
ISBN-10: 0-486-80519-0

Manufactured in the United States by RR Donnelley
80519001   2016
www.doverpublications.com

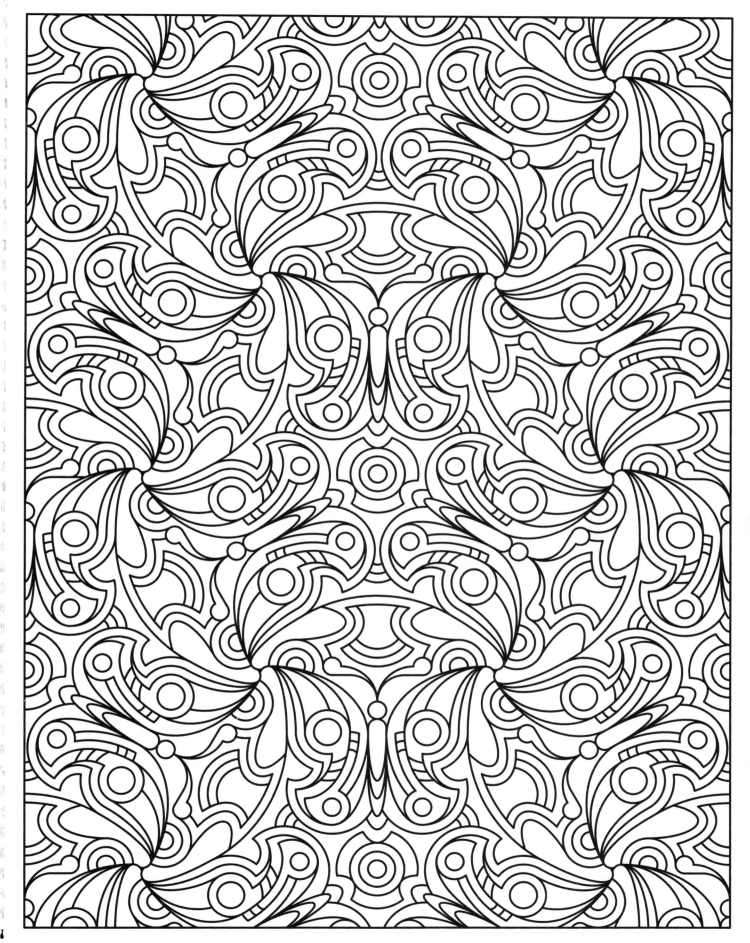

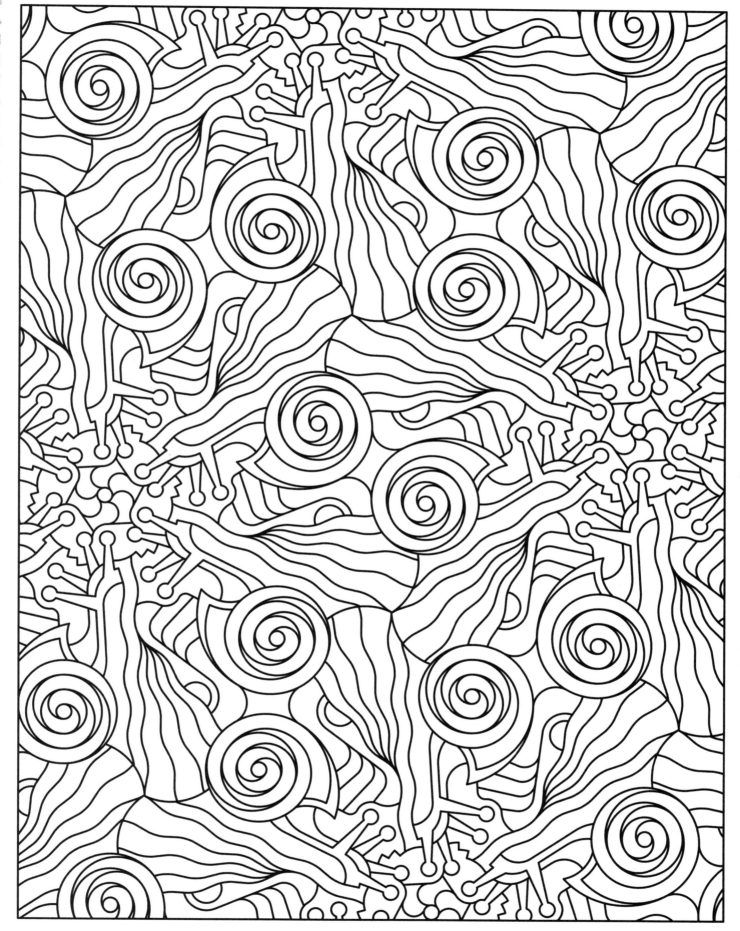

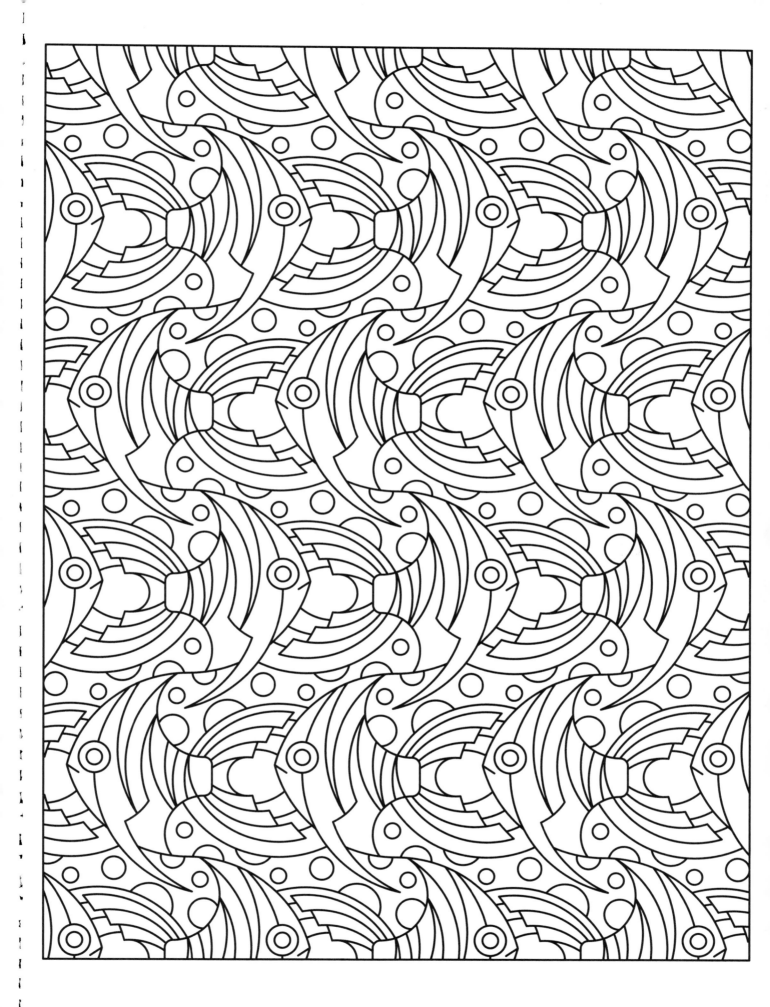

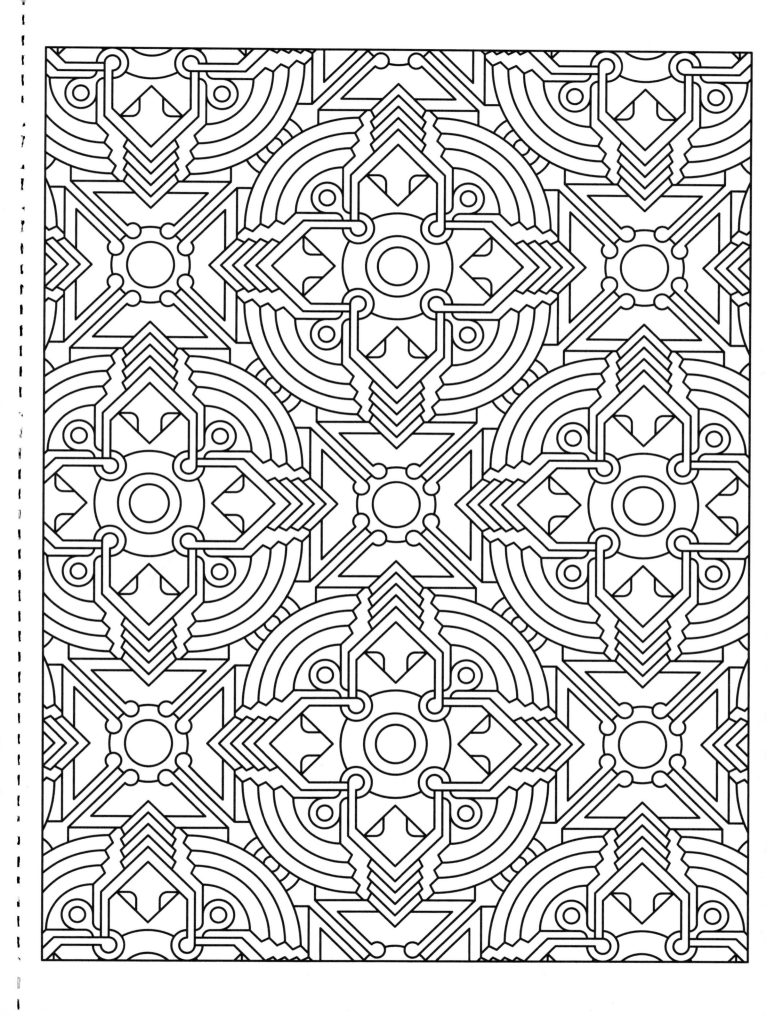

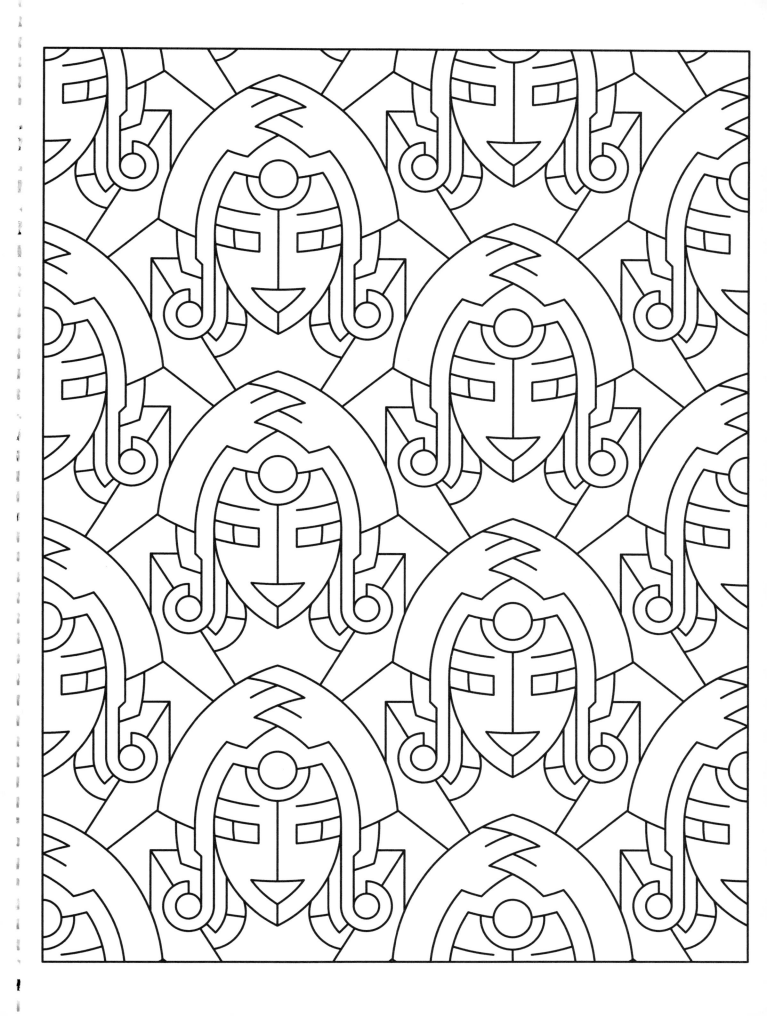

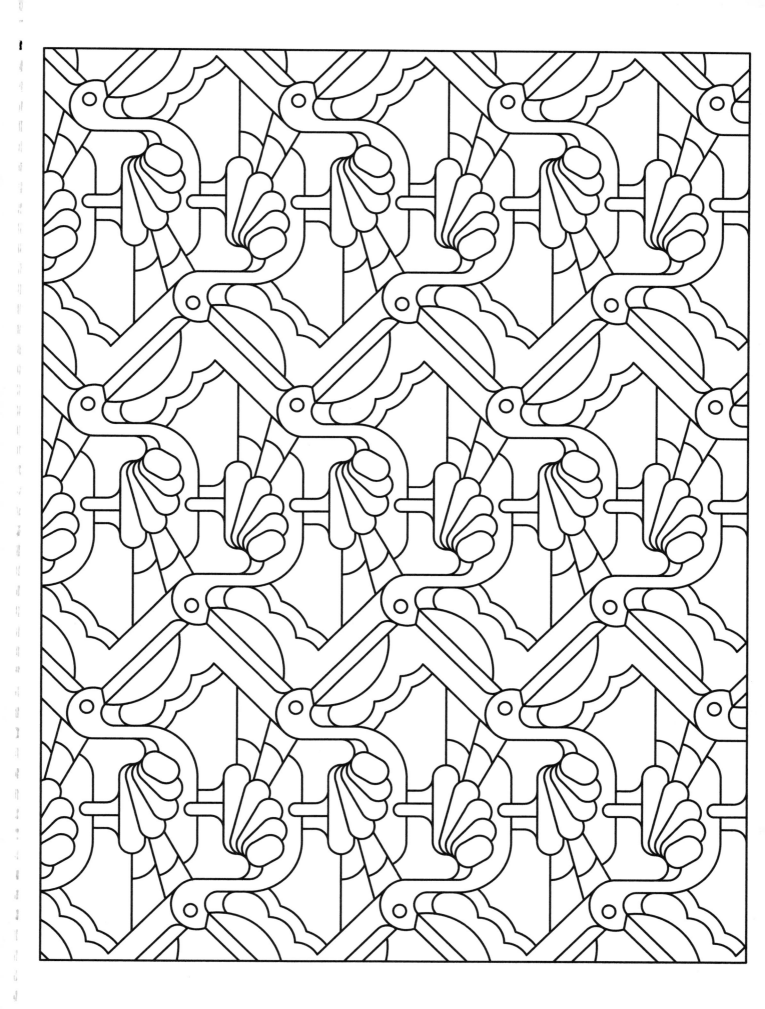

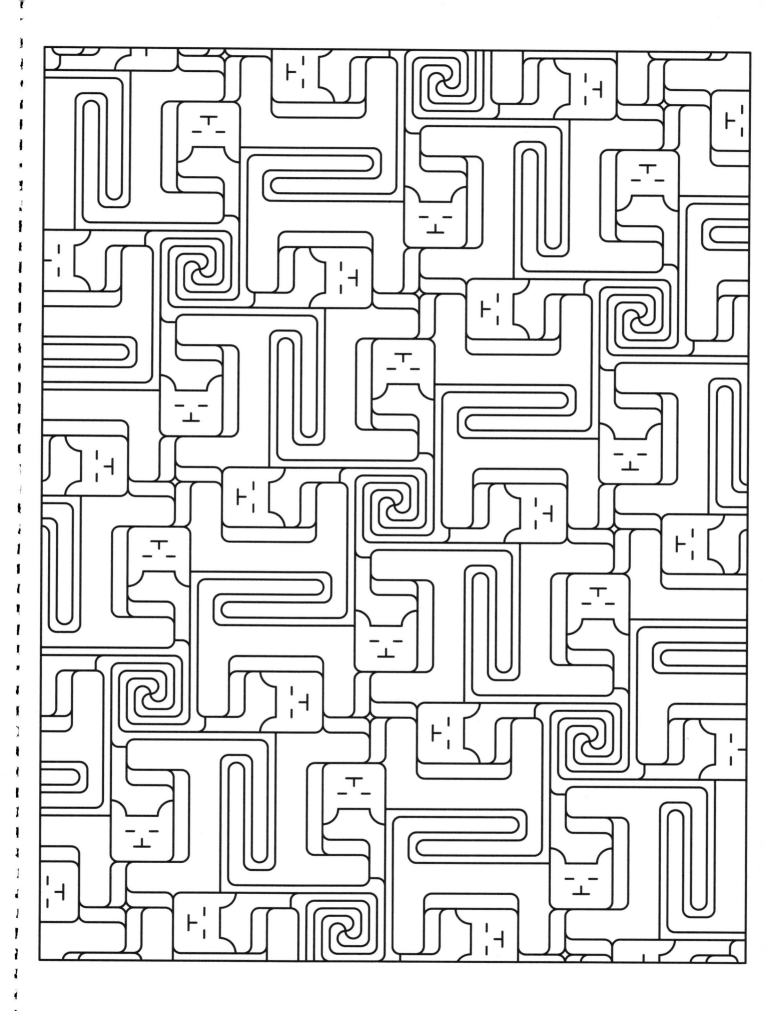

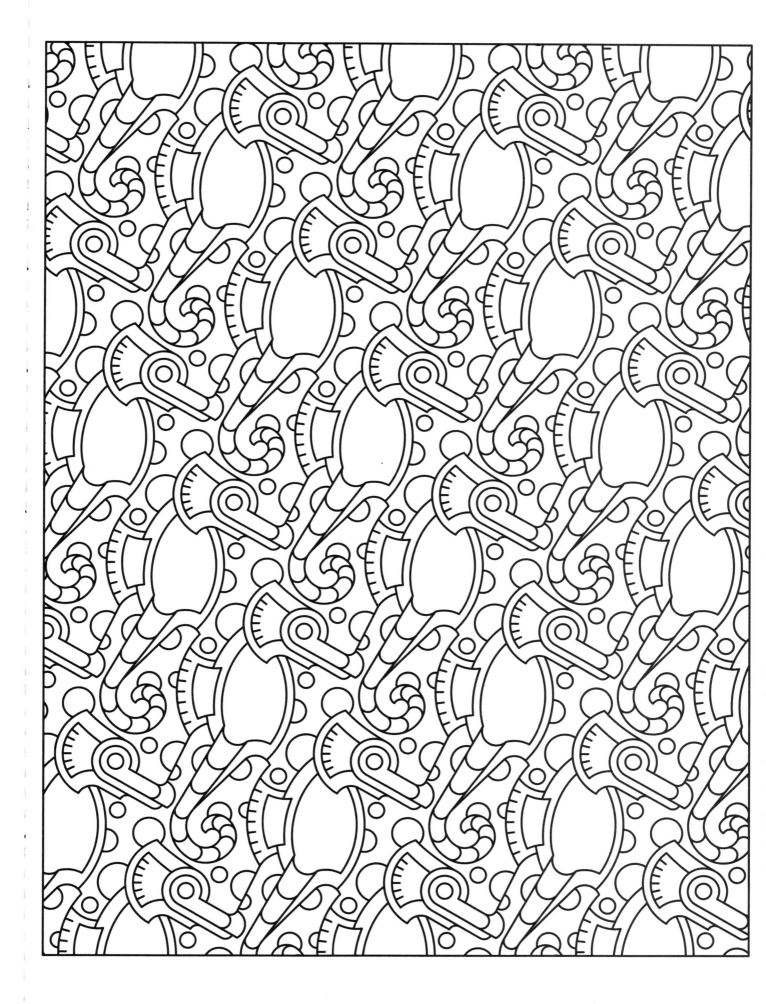

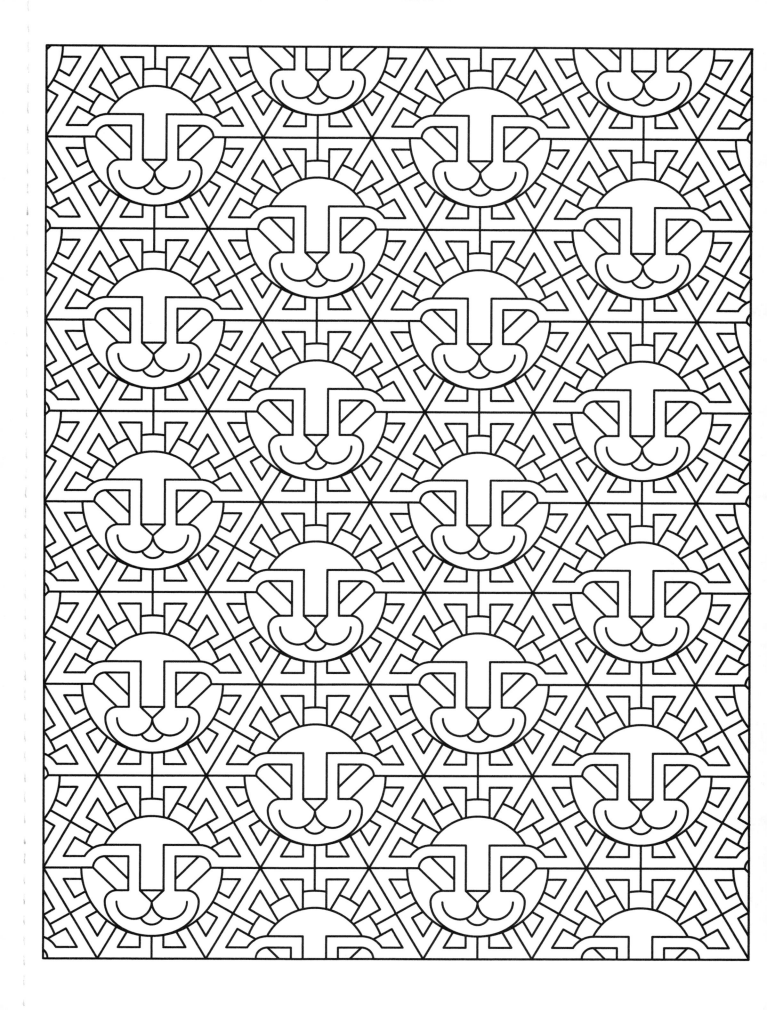

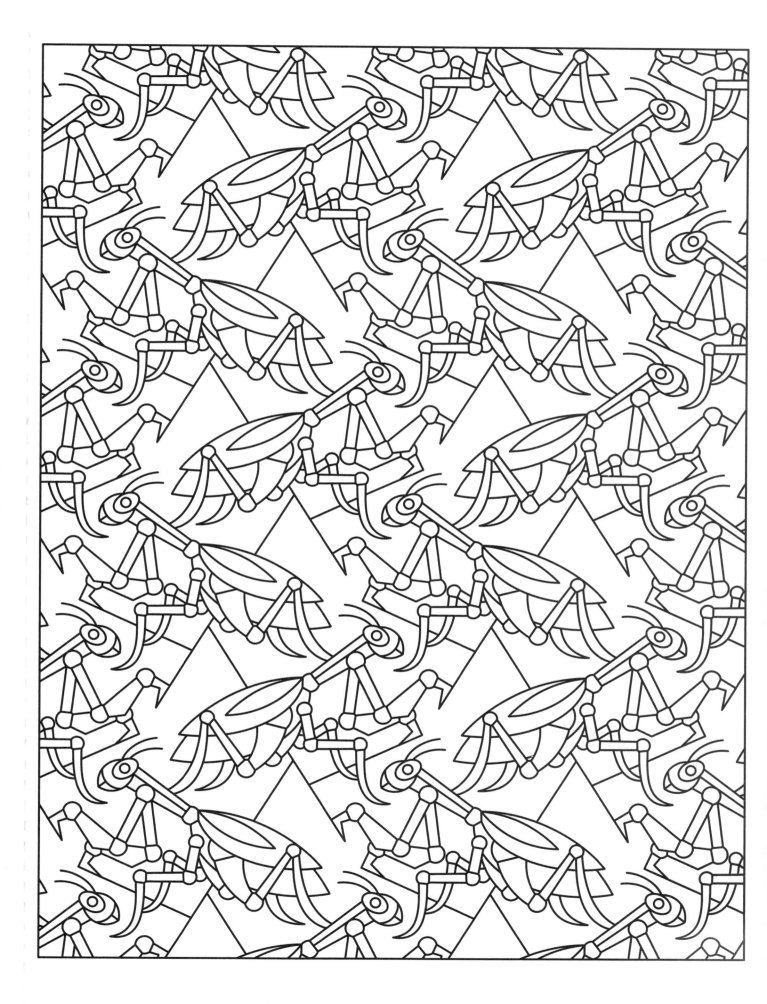

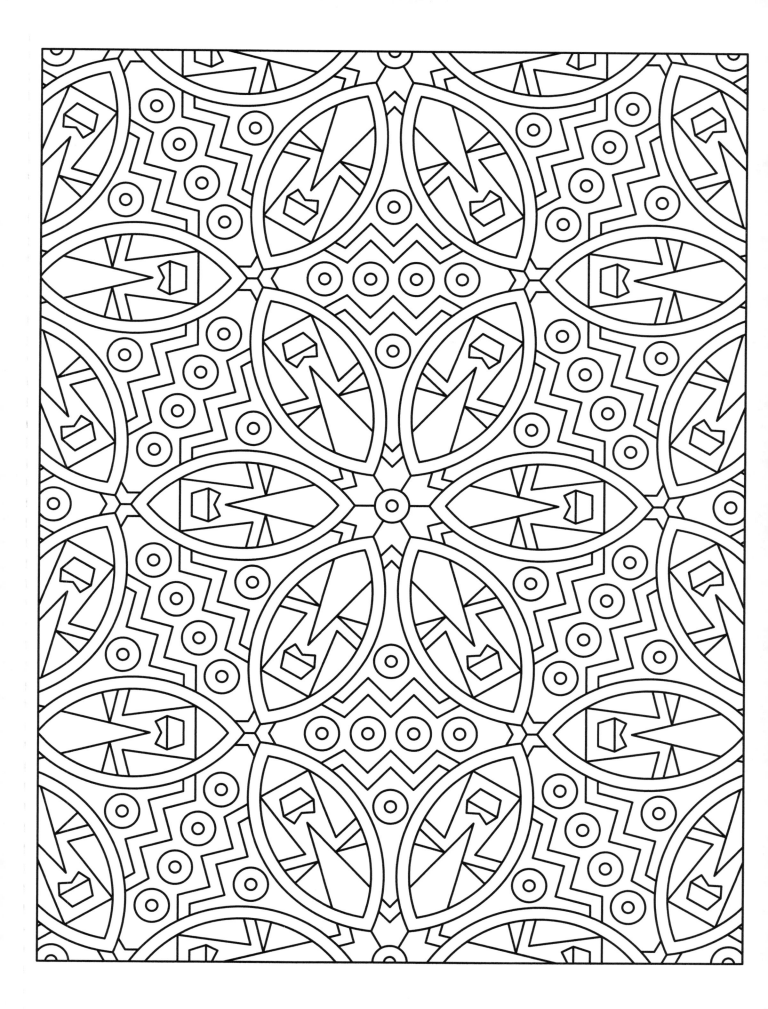

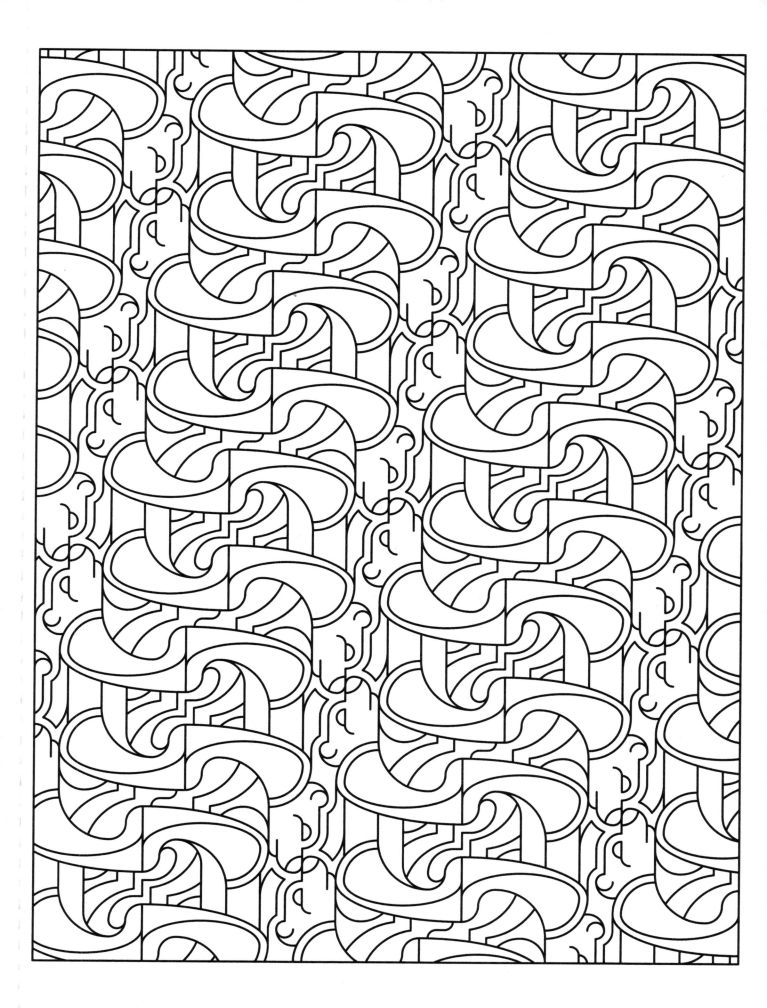

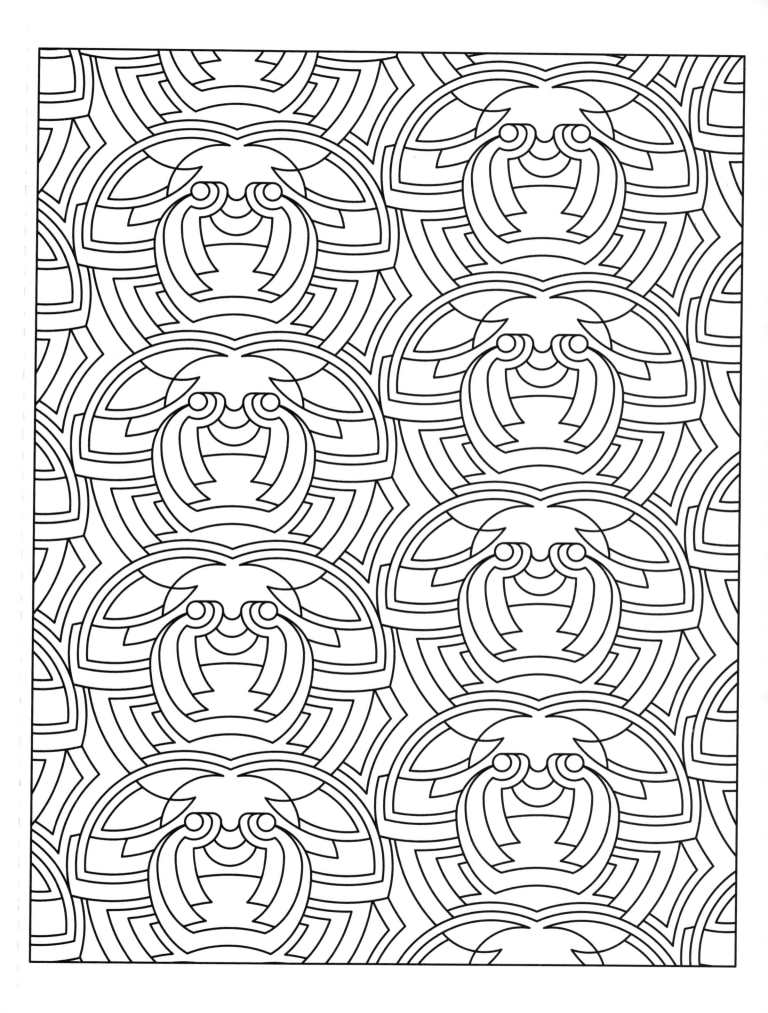

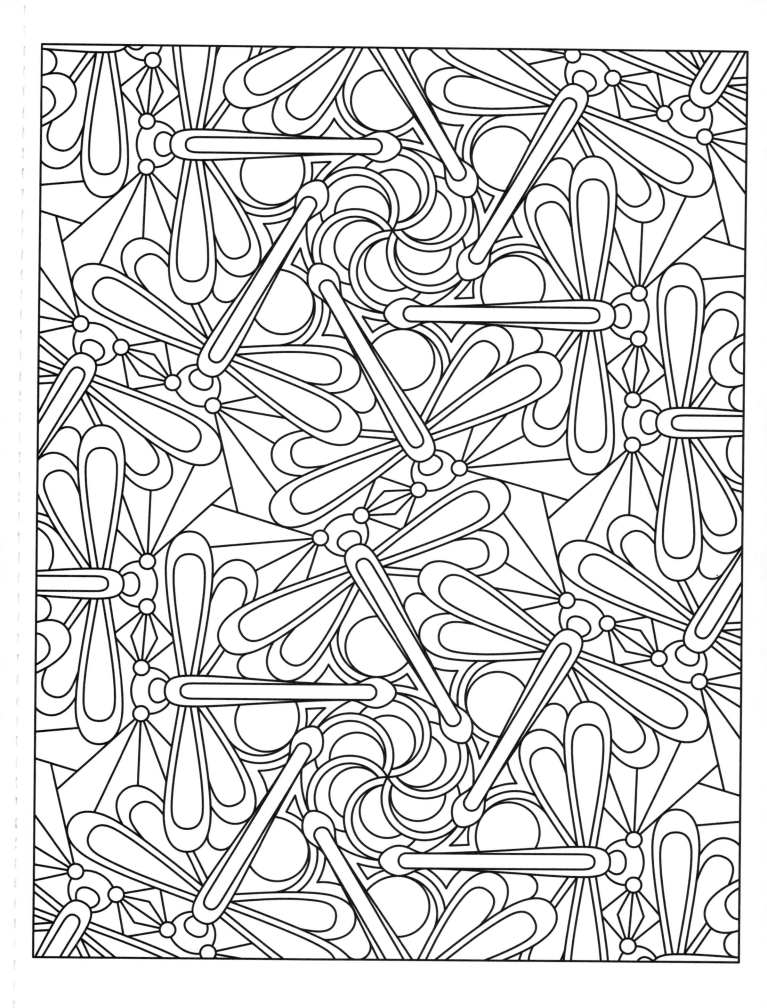

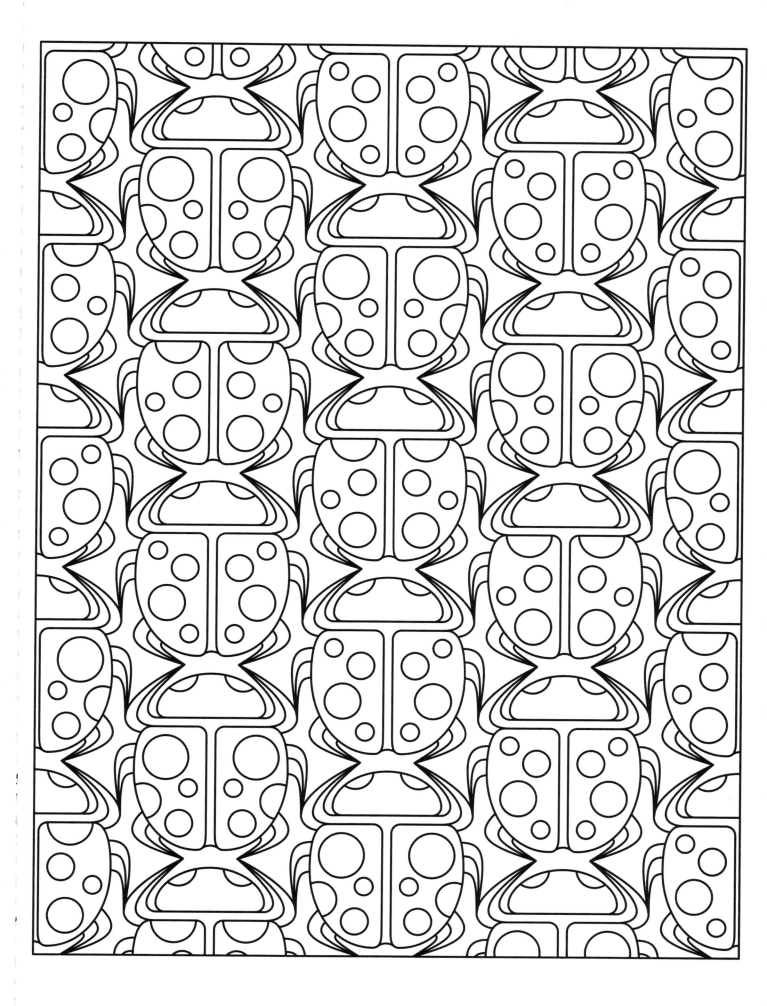

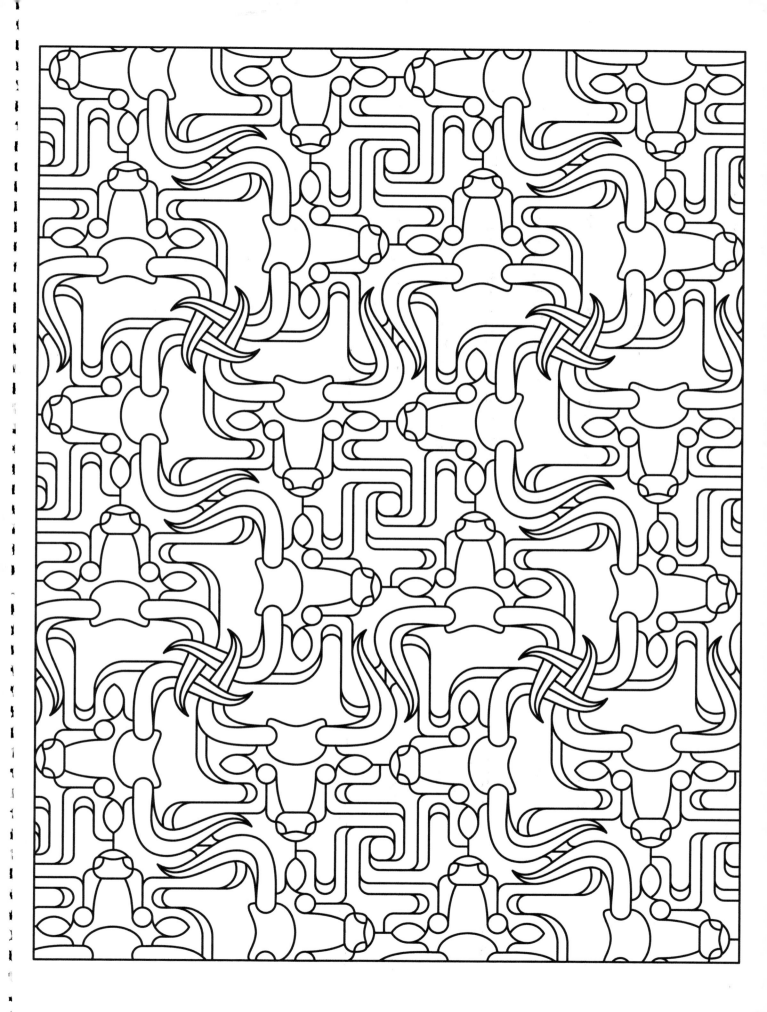

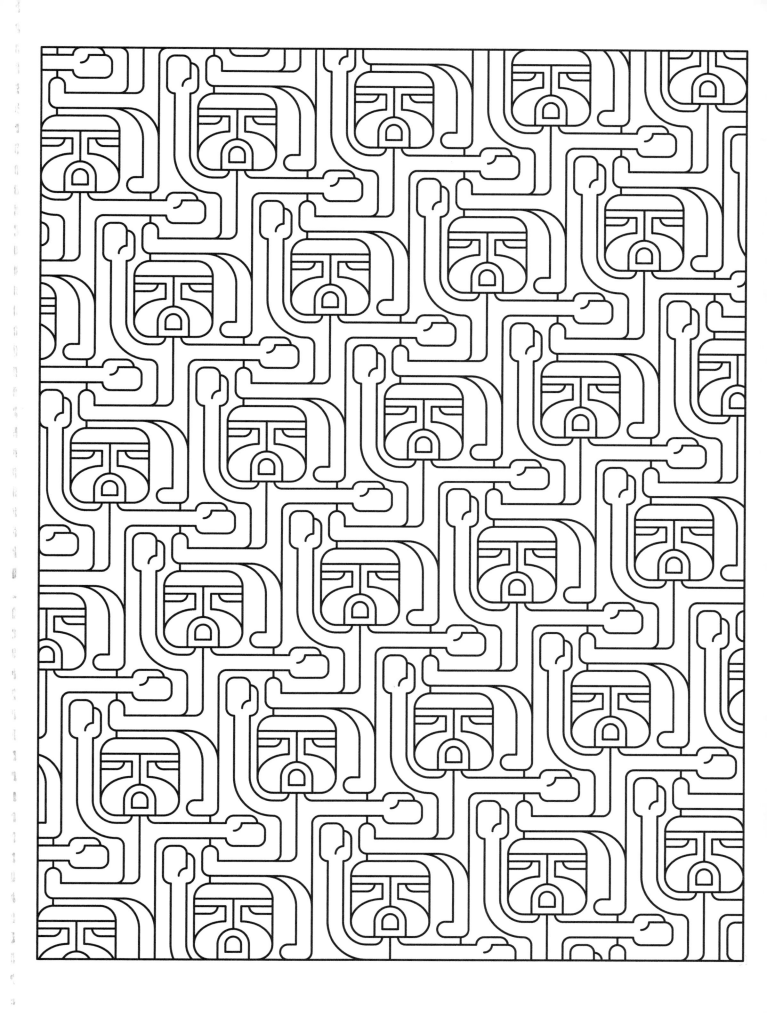

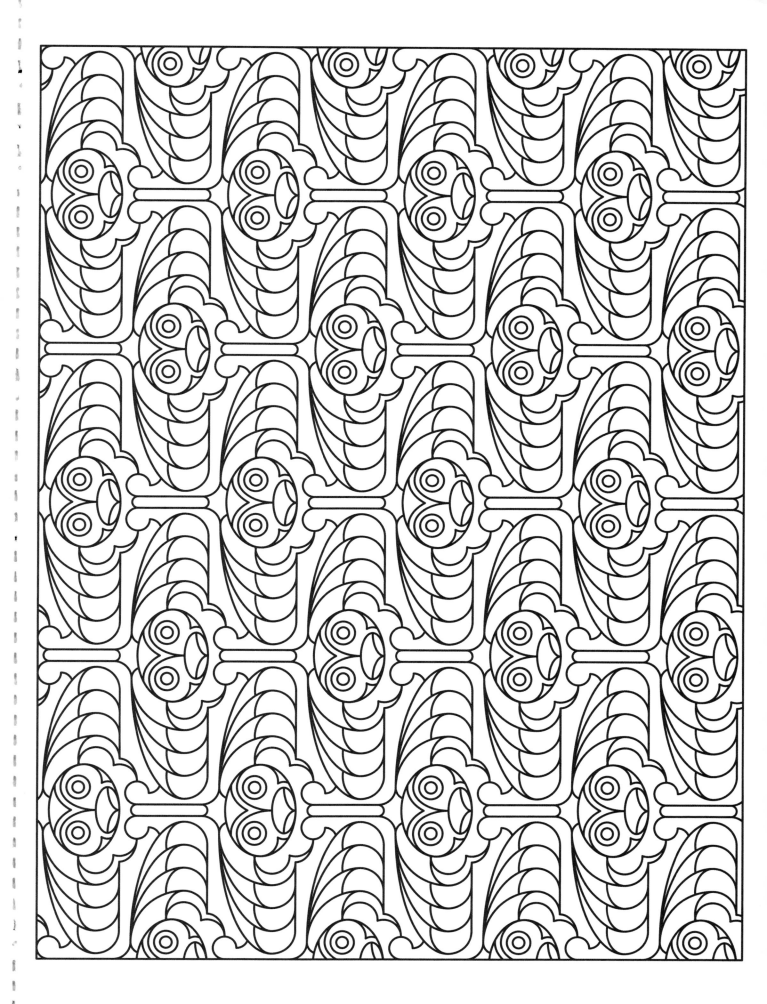

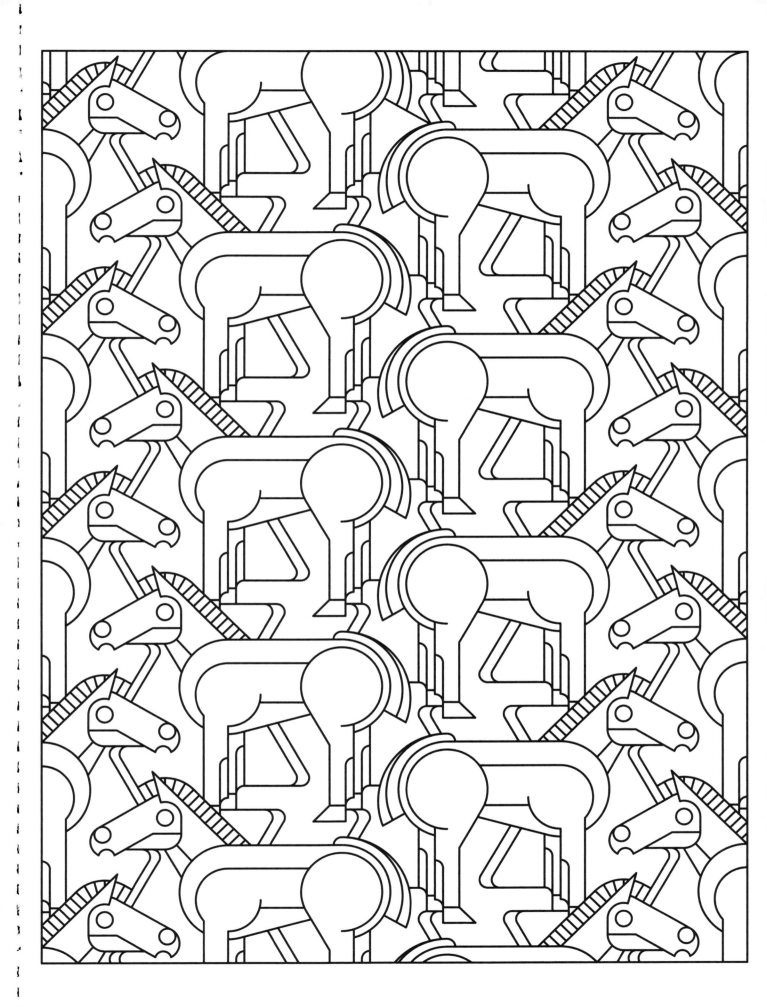

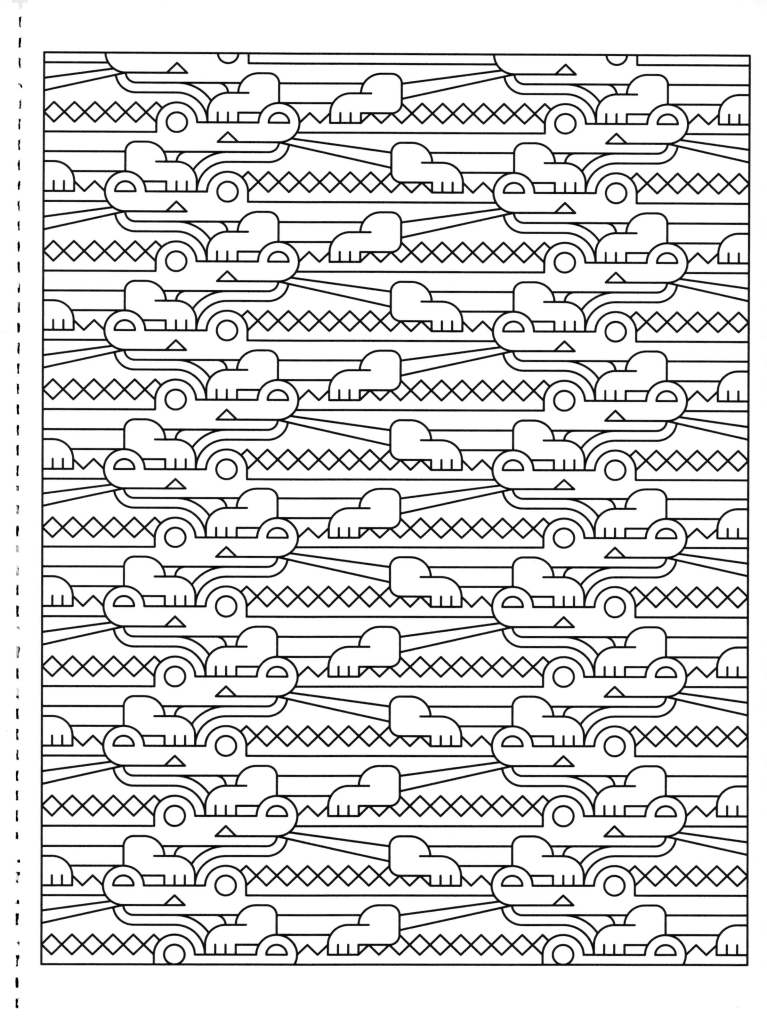

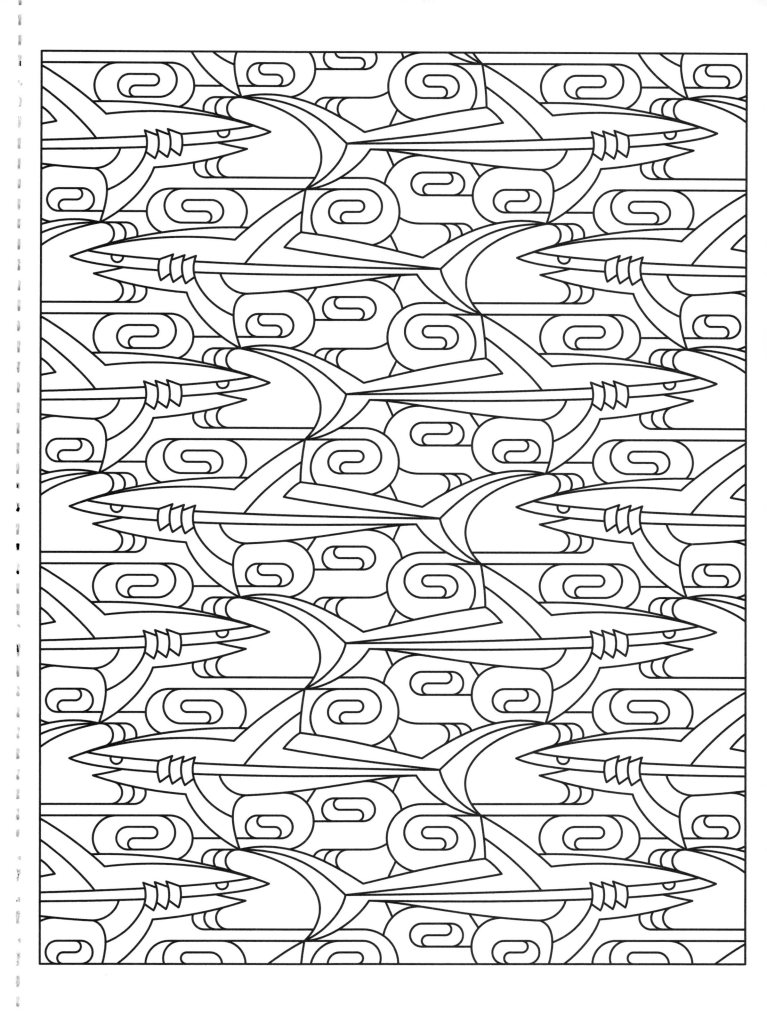

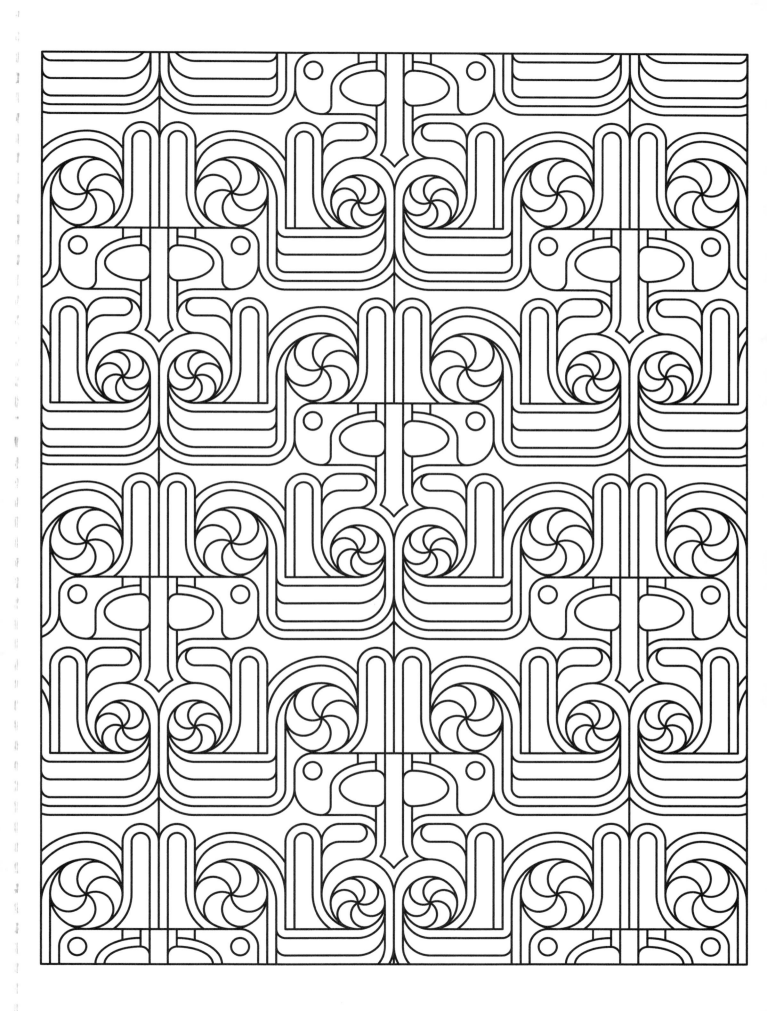

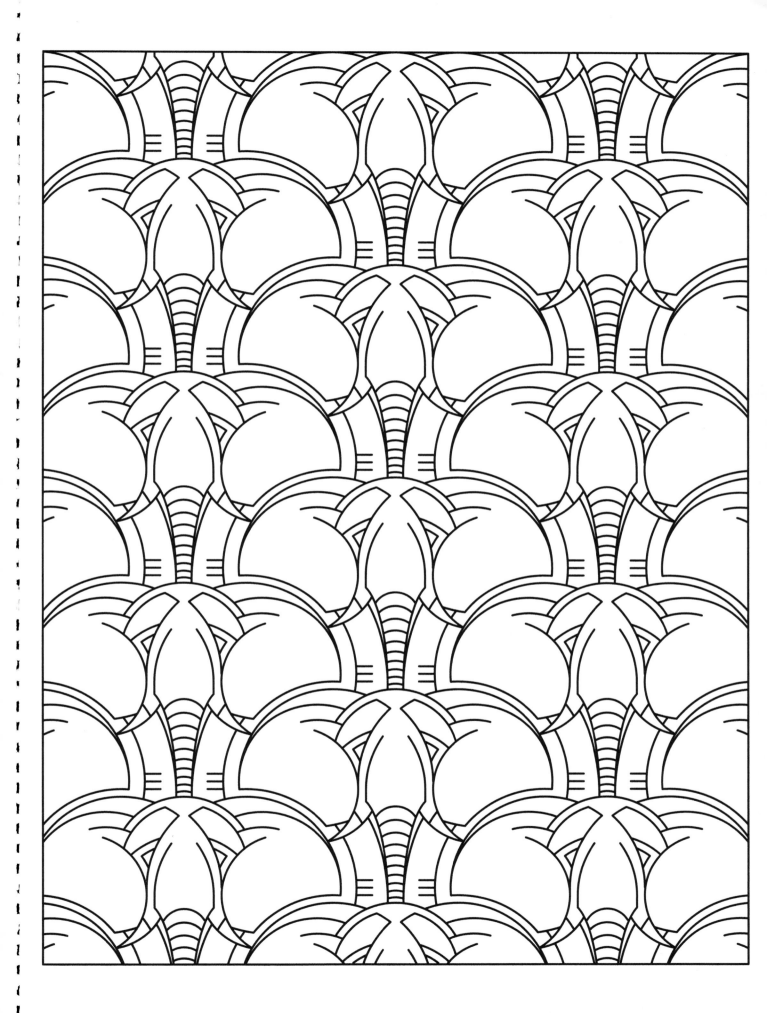

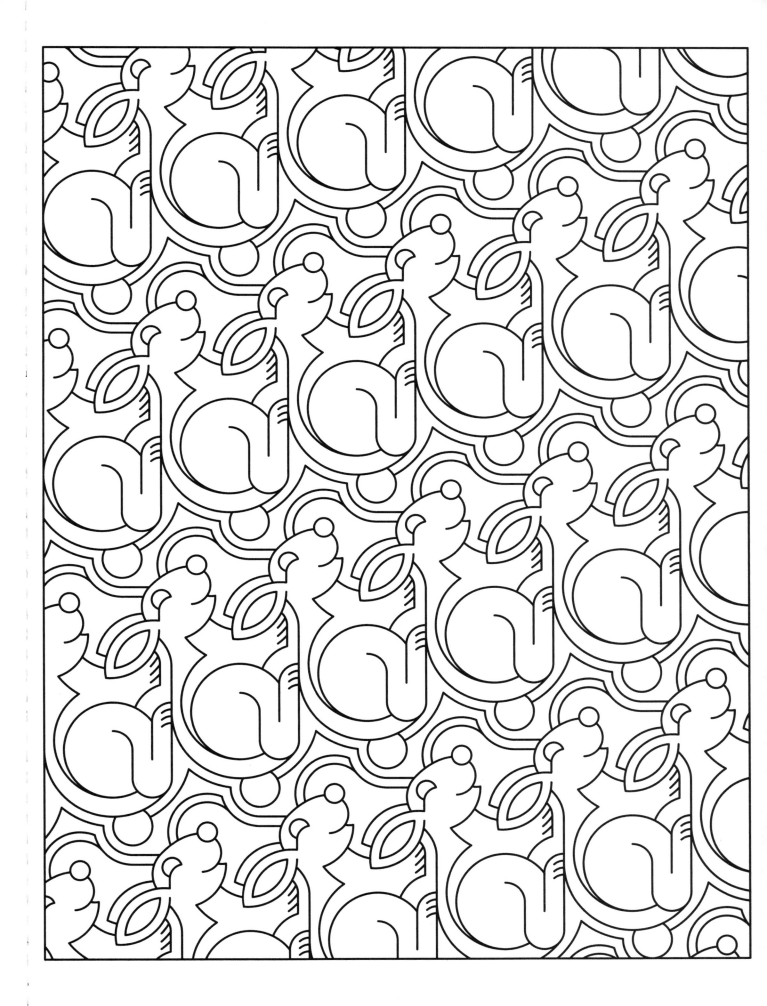

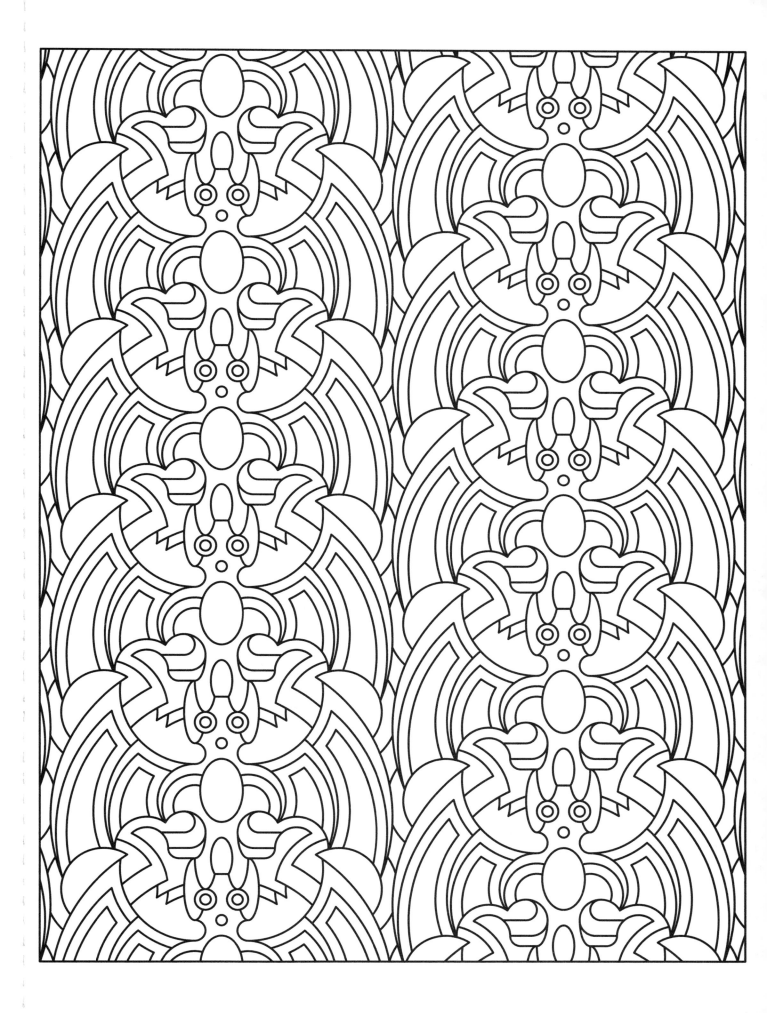

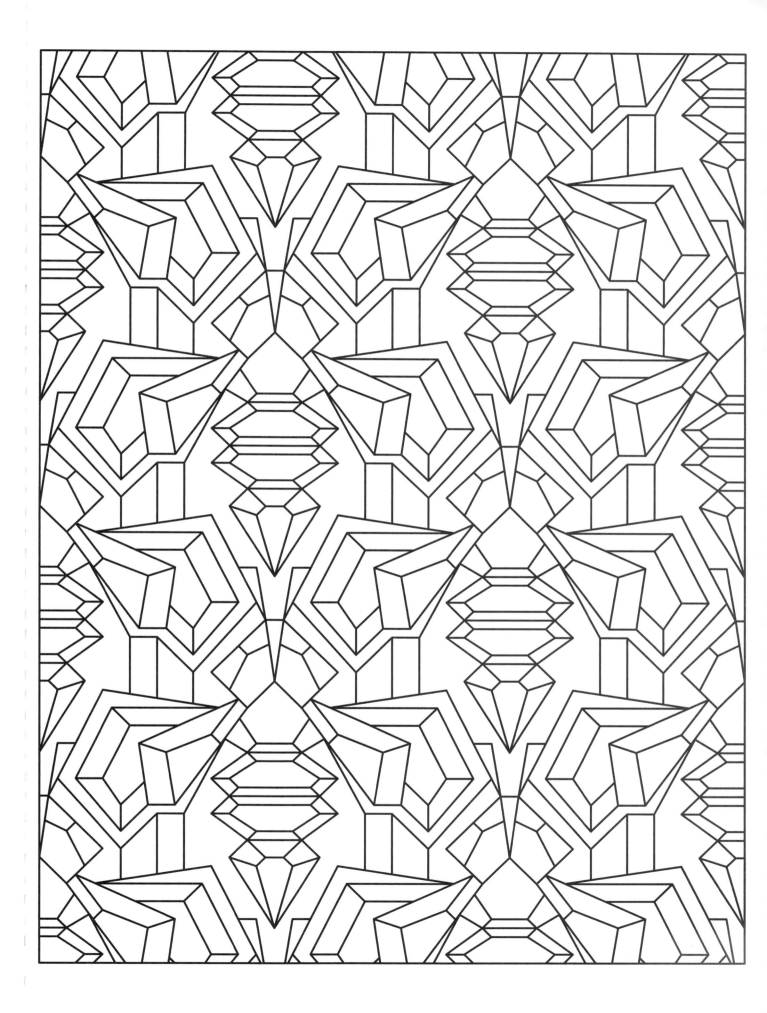

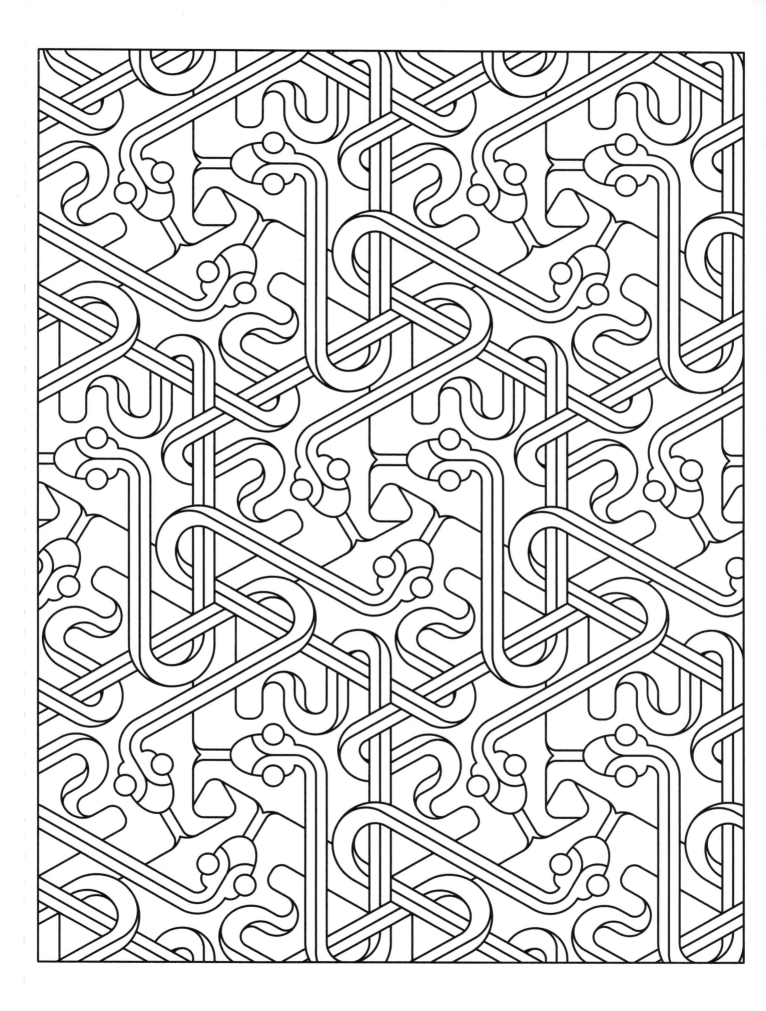

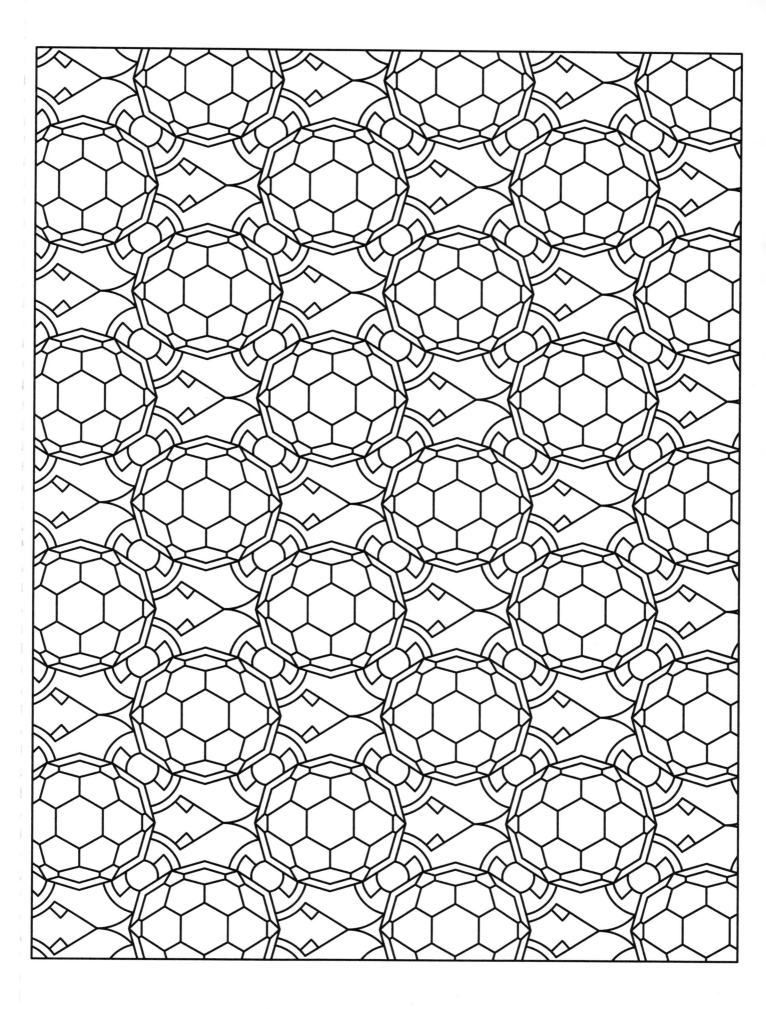

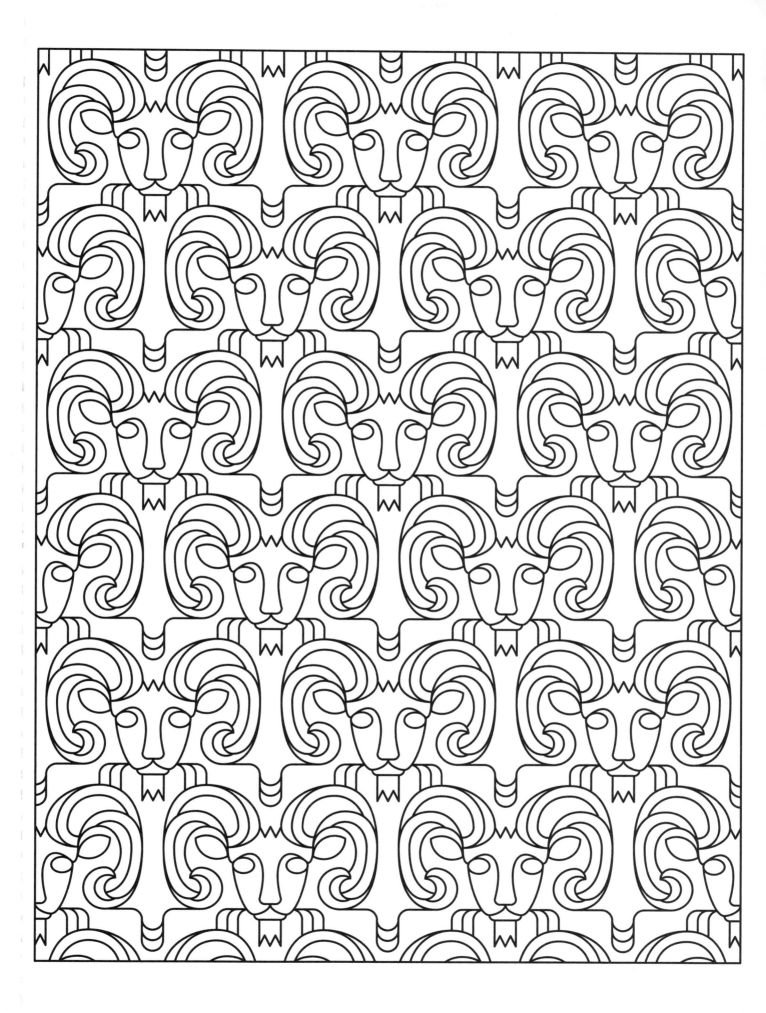

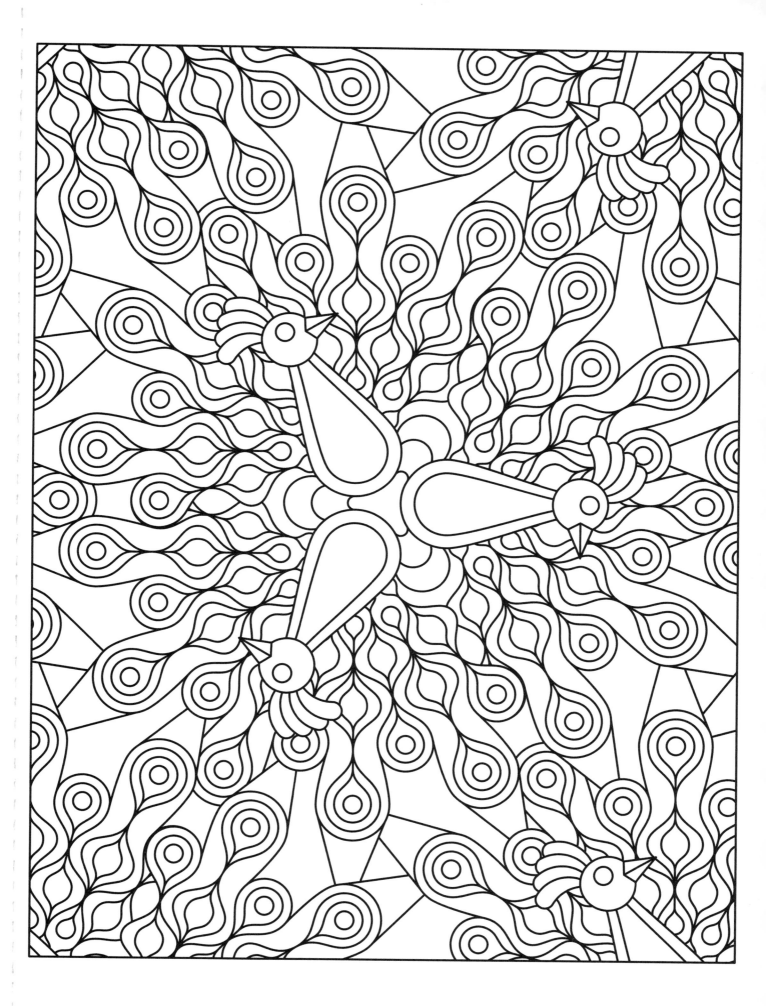

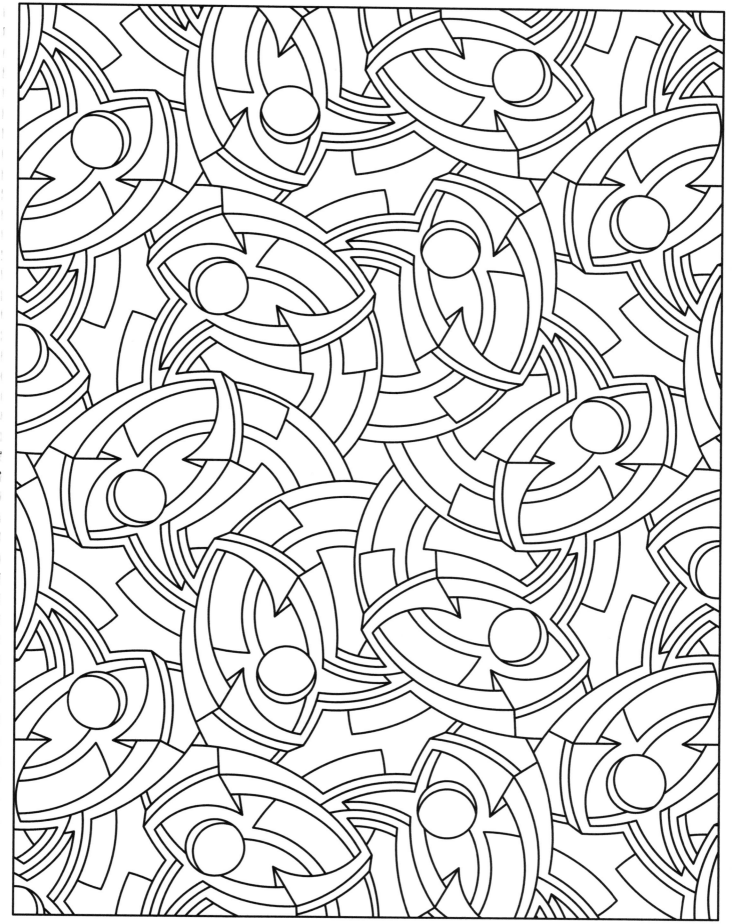